GW00500195

REST & WAR

A FIELD GUIDE FOR THE SPIRITUAL LIFE

STUDY GUIDE | SIX SESSIONS

BEN STUART

HarperChristian Resources

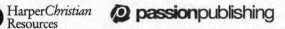
passionpublishing

Rest & War Study Guide
© 2022 by Ben Stuart

Requests for information should be addressed to:
HarperChristian Resources, 3900 Sparks Dr. SE, Grand Rapids, Michigan 49546

ISBN 978-0-310-14164-8 (softcover)
ISBN 978-0-310-14165-5 (ebook)

All Scripture quotations, unless otherwise indicated, are taken from the Holy Bible, New International Version®, NIV®. Copyright © 1973, 1978, 1984, 2011 by Biblica, Inc. ® Used by permission. All rights reserved worldwide.

Scripture quotations marked ESV are taken from The Holy Bible, English Standard Version. ESV® Text Edition: 2016. Copyright © 2001 by Crossway Bibles, a publishing ministry of Good News Publishers.

Scripture quotations marked KJV are taken from the King James Version.

Scripture quotations marked NASB are taken from the New American Standard Bible®, Copyright © 1960, 1971, 1977, 1995, 2020 by The Lockman Foundation. All rights reserved.

Scripture quotations marked NKJV are taken from the New King James Version®. Copyright © 1982 by Thomas Nelson. Used by permission. All rights reserved.

Any internet addresses (websites, blogs, etc.) and telephone numbers in this study guide are offered as a resource. They are not intended in any way to be or imply an endorsement by HarperChristian Resources, nor does HarperChristian Resources vouch for the content of these sites and numbers for the life of this study guide.

All rights reserved. No portion of this book may be reproduced, stored in a retrieval system, or transmitted in any form or by any means—electronic, mechanical, photocopy, recording, scanning, or other—except for brief quotations in critical reviews or articles, without the prior written permission of the publisher.

HarperChristian Resources titles may be purchased in bulk for church, business, fundraising, or ministry use. For information, please e-mail ResourceSpecialist@ChurchSource.com.

Published in partnership with Passion Publishing, LLC

First Printing July 2022 / Printed in the United States of America

CONTENTS

RHYTHMS OF A WELL-FOUGHT LIFE

REST
& WAR

AUTHORED BY BEN STUART

HOW TO USE THIS GUIDE

GROUP SIZE

This six-session video Bible study is designed to be experienced in a group setting such as a Bible study, Sunday school class, or other small-group gathering. If your gathering is large, you may want to consider splitting everyone into smaller groups of five or six people. This will ensure that everyone has enough time to participate in discussions.

MATERIALS NEEDED

Everyone in your group will need a copy of this study guide, which includes the opening questions to discuss, notes for the video teachings, directions for activities and discussion questions, and personal studies in between sessions. We also encourage you to get a copy of the book *Rest & War*, which will provide further insights into the material you are covering in this study. To aid your study experience, you will be asked to read specific chapters in the book to prepare for the group's next meeting.

FACILITATION

Your group will need to appoint a person to serve as a facilitator. This person will be responsible for starting the video and keeping track of time during discussions and activities. Facilitators may also read questions aloud and monitor discussions, prompting everyone in the group to respond and assuring that everyone has the opportunity to participate. If you have been chosen for this role, note that there are additional instructions and resources in the back of this guide to help you lead your group members through the study.

PERSONAL STUDIES

During the week, you can maximize the impact of this course with the personal studies provided. Treat each personal study like a devotional and use them in whatever way works best for your schedule. You could do one section each day for three days of the week or complete them all in one sitting. These personal studies are not intended to be burdensome or time-consuming but to provide a richer experience and continuity in between your group sessions.

INTRODUCTION

"Oh God, we are so stupid." These were the first words of my friend's prayer. I don't remember his next few lines, because my eyes were scanning the snow-covered mountains under our perch high atop Longs Peak. As we sat there, entirely depleted, I wondered, *How long until our friends file a missing person's report?* I knew for certain there was no way that we could get down that mountain using only our internal resources.

It had started out well. I had joined a team of college students for a summer-long internship in Denver, Colorado. Early on, my friend had invited me to climb this massive four-teen-thousand-foot mountain. We began to train and resolved to summit Longs Peak one month later. At one point as the trail ascended, we both began to struggle for air. Each heave of our bodies required an enormous expenditure of energy.

But this was not the time to stop! We pushed ourselves on and reached a rocky path high above. From there, we followed the route around a corner . . . followed by another . . . until we came to another steep incline. At the sight of it, we both slumped to the ground. We were exhausted, nauseous, and *stuck*. After a few moments of listening to the wind whistle through the mountain range below, we began our prayer acknowledging our stupidity.

Then it happened. I saw a head pop out from behind a boulder. "Hey, guys!" a voice shouted. "Great day to hike! You guys been to the top yet?" The man stopped and surveyed us. "Wait a second, you're the college guys who came up here without equipment. We're in awe of you. You're crazy!" He then returned to his original question: "You been to the top?"

I told him we had not and were not planning to do so. "You have to go," he replied. "C'mon guys!" I stood up on my wobbly legs. "We are not doing well," I whispered. "We are totally exhausted. There is no way we can go any farther."

His demeanor changed. He set down his pack and produced two pairs of arm-length mittens. "First things first," he then said. "You are breathing wrong. You are in a new environment. The atmosphere has changed. You have to adapt if you want to survive."

I often think about this moment as I survey our world today. Shifts in the atmosphere of society have had an impact on our vibrancy and the way we interact with God. We are depleted, exhausted, nauseous, and stuck. We are distraught by the uncertainty and anxiety around us and by the fear, lust, pride, and doubt within us. We don't know how to manage it—and feel helpless. We need a guide to emerge who will show us how to move forward.

The good news is that we have such a Guide. He looks at us not with eyes of condemnation but with compassion. He has many things to teach us—if we have ears to listen.

What you will find in this study is not a scolding for your struggles nor a motivational speech to try harder. I want to bring you to the Good Shepherd, show you the ancient path that leads to rest for your soul, and equip you to advance toward your God-given destiny.

This is a call to battle and to build—to *war* against the Enemy so you can find *rest* for your soul. I'm not talking about fighting skirmishes for your ego or building flimsy kingdoms that fall like a house of cards. I'm talking about expending your maximum energy for the greatest of all causes. I want you to fight the battle of the ages and build a kingdom that will never fade.

The challenge is before you. *Are you ready to accept it?* Let's jump in and begin.

—BEN STUART

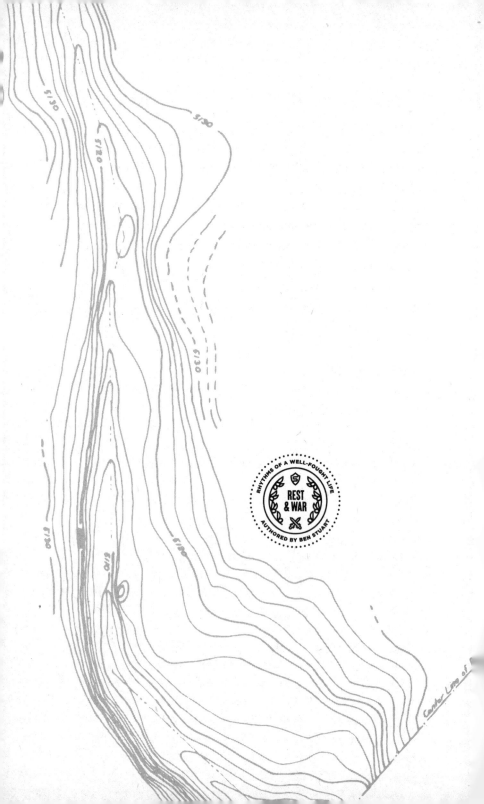

RHYTHMS OF A WELL-FOUGHT LIFE

REST
& WAR

AUTHORED BY BEN STUART

FREED TO FIGHT

Consider him who endured from sinners such hostility against himself, so that you may not grow weary or fainthearted.

HEBREWS 12:3 ESV

WELCOME

"I'm just glad I made it."

What? I couldn't believe what I was hearing.

I was visiting with a mentor who had just transitioned well from leading one successful ministry to leading another. As a young minister, I asked him how it felt to retire after building a thriving ministry. I thought he would talk about how rewarding it was to impact so many lives or share some of the secret strategies of his success. I did not expect him to express gratitude for *survival*.

But then I thought about my own experience. I watched two ministers I knew lose their families and ministries because of infidelity. I observed others plunge into depression after years of maintaining an unsustainable schedule. As I surveyed the wreckage of broken relationships, shattered hearts, and demolished dreams, suddenly my mentor's assessment made much more sense. To succeed, we need to learn how to survive.

Many of us enter into our adult lives with a swell of optimism. We want to use the gifts and abilities we possess to make our mark on the world! But then we encounter difficulties and discouragements all around us. We also discover all manner of insecurities, fears, lusts, and addictions within us. How do we avoid being crushed by the chaos which abounds not only out in the world but also inside of us?

The writer of Hebrews charges us, "Let us also lay aside every weight, and sin which clings so closely, and let us run with endurance the race that is set before us, looking to Jesus, the founder and perfecter of our faith, who for the joy that was set before him endured the cross" (Hebrews 12:1–2 ESV).

We do have a race to run that our Maker has marked out for us. A life of meaning awaits us. And this will require that we disentangle ourselves from ways of thinking and living that will derail our God-given purpose. But notice before we wrestle and before we run, we need to watch what Jesus has done on our behalf. Before we begin the fight, we need to understand how we've been fought for.

Ben Sherwood wrote a book years ago on survival called *The Survivor's Club*. He sets out to explain, given the inevitability of adversity, who survives and thrives. Which is the safest seat on an airplane? Where is the best place to have a heart attack? In the book, he includes a chapter on faith, even though he admits he did not want to do so. He was not interested in the subject but found that God came up so often in stories of survival that he had to address the topic. In preparation for writing, he interviewed the man who had literally written the book on survival, *How to Survive on Land and Sea*, for the Naval Survival Training institute. Ben asked this former marine-drill instructor, "What is the secret to survival?" The man answered without hesitation, "Faith in God. It is a major factor in all survival scenarios." He felt so strongly about this that he opened his survival manual with the words of Psalm 23: Yea, though I walk through the valley of the shadow of death, I will fear no evil: for thou art with me" (verse 4 KJV).[1]

Before we engage in learning the strategies and tactics we need to survive and thrive in our spiritual lives, we must first fix our eyes on the God who fought for us. The greatest fighters are those who know they have been fought for. So, before we hack our way through the wilderness, we need to look at the Trailblazer who made a way for us!

SHARE

Before we jump into this session, take a few minutes to introduce yourself to anyone you haven't met yet in the group. Then, to get things started, discuss one of the following questions:

➤ How do you respond to the idea that spirituality is a struggle?

— *or* —

➤ What does it mean for you to keep your eyes fixed on Christ?

READ

Invite someone to read aloud the following passage. Listen for fresh insights as you hear the verses being read and then discuss the questions that follow.

> *Dear children, do not let anyone lead you astray. The one who does what is right is righteous, just as he is righteous. The one who does what is sinful is of the devil, because the devil has been sinning from the beginning. The reason the Son of God appeared was to destroy the devil's work. No one who is born of God will continue to sin, because God's seed remains in them; they cannot go on sinning, because they have been born of God. This is how we know who the children of God are and who the children of the devil are: Anyone who does not do what is right is not God's child, nor is anyone who does not love their brother and sister.*

> 1 JOHN 3:7-10

What does John say is the reason that Jesus came to earth?

What do you find unsettling in this passage? What questions would you want to ask John?

WATCH

Play the video segment for session one (use the streaming video access provided on the inside front cover). As you watch, use the following outline to record any thoughts or concepts that stand out to you.

Like a solider dropped behind enemy lines, "The Son of God appeared for this purpose, to destroy the works of the devil" (1 John 3:8 NASB). The reason we celebrate Christmas is because God wanted something destroyed—the Enemy of our soul.

God has established physical, relational, moral, and spiritual laws by which his world is governed. But the devil wants to overthrow God's laws and lead us into spiritual anarchy.

God saw humanity disobey him and knew the devastation it would bring. But he told the deceiver, "I will put enmity between you and the woman, and between your seed and her Seed; He shall bruise your head, and you shall bruise His heel" (Genesis 3:15 NKJV). Theologians call this the *protoevangelium*, the first gospel, a declaration of the good news of a savior.

Jesus proclaimed, "The Spirit of the Lord is upon me, because he has anointed me to proclaim good news to the poor. He has sent me to proclaim liberty to the captives . . . to set at liberty those who are oppressed" (Luke 4:18 ESV). He stepped out to do damage against the darkness.

Jesus explained his ministry this way: "When a strong man, fully armed, guards his own house, his possessions are safe. But when someone stronger attacks and overpowers him, he takes away the armor in which the man trusted and divides up his plunder" (Luke 11:21–22). He came to destroy the "strong one"—the devil—and set us free.

Jesus destroyed the works of the devil not by perpetrating violence, but by taking violence upon himself. He overcame the Enemy's greatest weapon—our just condemnation for our sin—by becoming human, taking our condemnation for us, and rising victoriously from the grave (see Hebrews 2:14–15).

Jesus has led a triumph, and we are victorious. The aroma of his victory permeates us: "But thanks be to God, who in Christ always leads us in triumphal procession, and through us spreads the fragrance of the knowledge of him everywhere" (2 Corinthians 2:14 ESV).

You have been liberated and freed to *fight.* Jesus has won the decisive victory. Your sin has been canceled. Your debt has been paid. You are loved by a holy God. Victory is your destiny. Let this truth embolden you to pursue the victory that he has purchased for us all.

DISCUSS

Take a few minutes within your group to discuss the message and explore these concepts in Scripture.

1. How does considering Jesus' mission—"to destroy the devil's work" (1 John 3:8)—change the way you view your relationship with God? How does it change your view of what it means to follow after Christ?

2. How was destroying the works of the devil part of God's plan from the beginning? Why was this necessary in light of Adam and Eve's disobedience?

3. What are the implications for your own struggles when you consider that Jesus has the power to take away the devil's weapons of destruction?

4. When have you experienced this kind of power in your life most recently?

5. How can you celebrate—both individually and communally—the triumph of Jesus' victory over sin and death? How does celebrating this victory empower you to experience freedom in the midst of struggles?

6. What is one area of your life where you would like to experience greater victory?

RESPOND

As you reflect on the group discussion and what you will take away from this session, consider what it means for you to experience victory over the struggles you face most frequently. To facilitate this process, at the end of each session you will find an exercise to help you apply the teaching so you can experience rest and battle more effectively in your life. This exercise is also meant to be a way to help others in your group as you learn and grow together.

In this first session, you have started the process of exploring what it means to reconsider your spiritual battles and embrace the power that Christ has made available to you. Taking inventory of where you are spiritually is a good way to begin. Toward this goal, spend a few minutes answering the following questions in the space provided. Remember, no one will see your responses unless you choose to share them.

What stands out in this session that seems especially true right now in your life? How do you see this truth manifesting itself in your present circumstances?

As you consider what it means to engage in spiritual war to live in the freedom Jesus has won, where do you feel most vulnerable? What are your areas of weakness right now?

Finally, what are your expectations for this group study? How can the group help you grow in your faith and draw closer to God?

Review your answers and ask God to meet you where you are at this time.

PRAY

Conclude your session by sharing any requests you would like the group to lift up in prayer. Thank God for bringing you together for this study so that you can help and encourage one another as you seek to recognize and overcome the Enemy's snares. Ask God to give you clarity, wisdom, and discernment as you proceed into this group study. Trust that your Good Shepherd will guide you to rest and equip you for overcoming trials and temptations.

PERSONAL STUDY

This week's group discussion is just the start! We want you to continue digging into these concepts throughout the week ahead. So, we've created this section as a guide for your personal study time to further explore the topics you discussed with your group. Before you begin, review chapters 1 and 2 in *Rest & War*. Note there will be an opportunity at your next group session to share any responses or thoughts that you have.

CONNECT

Check in with your group members during the upcoming week and continue the discussion you had with them at your last gathering. Grab coffee or dinner or reach out by text and share what's going on in your heart. Use the following questions to help guide your conversation.

What are some key words and phrases that have continued to stand out to you from your last group session? Why have those especially resonated with you?

What does it mean in your present season of life that you have been "freed to fight"? What is the greatest battle that you are facing right now?

When have you experienced God's presence in the midst of your daily battles? How does knowing he is with you make a difference when you encounter unexpected problems?

REFLECT

Take a moment and read Titus 2:11–14:

> For the grace of God has appeared, bringing salvation for all people, training us to renounce ungodliness and worldly passions, and to live self-controlled, upright, and godly lives in the present age, waiting for our blessed hope, the appearing of the glory of our great God and Savior Jesus Christ, who gave himself for us to redeem us from all lawlessness and to purify for himself a people for his own possession who are zealous for good works (ESV).

What stands out to you? Why?

In this passage, Paul explains that the grace of God accomplishes two things. First, it brings salvation. Because of the appearance of God's kindness, rescue from the penalty of sin is now available to all who place their faith in Jesus. No one earns redemption here. The kindness of God makes rescue available to all, no matter what we may have done in life.

But the kindness of God does not just bring rescue; it also trains us! It is the grace of God that teaches us to let go of the destructive ways of living that were once the hallmarks of our previous existence. The kindness of God teaches us to live in an appropriate way as we deal with God, others, and ourselves.

This is important: God does not shame us into life change. He loves us into it. We do not work to earn God's approval. We work because we have it. His love precedes and prompts our life change! Because he redeemed us from destructive ways of living and thinking, we can renounce them. We can fight because he fought for us.

How does knowing that Jesus "gave himself for us to redeem us" reframe how you think about the sin in your life?

Does the knowledge that you are loved by God motivate you to want to renounce destructive ways of thinking and living? Why or why not?

Do you think of God as a gracious teacher and trainer or as a perpetually disappointed father? How might this shift of perspective help you in your fight against sin in your own life?

WORSHIP

One of the Enemy's most common strategies is to cultivate discontent in your heart. It may be triggered from seeing someone else's social media post, a commercial on TV, or a conversation you overhear at work. The devil tries to convince you that everyone else has what you want—and what you *could* have—if only you are willing to disobey God and go your own way. This struggle is nothing new. In fact, the people of Israel often fell prey to this scheme, thanking God for his provision one day and then looking at their neighbors and complaining against God the next. In the following passage, the prophet Isaiah tried to get the people to see that their deepest longings could *never* be satisfied by earthly pursuits but only by drawing closer to God. Read through the passage and then spend a few minutes answering the questions that follow.

> *"Come, all you who are thirsty,*
>   *come to the waters;*
> *and you who have no money,*
>   *come, buy and eat!*
> *Come, buy wine and milk*
>   *without money and without cost.*
> *Why spend money on what is not bread,*
>   *and your labor on what does not satisfy?*
> *Listen, listen to me, and eat what is good,*
>   *and you will delight in the richest of fare.*
>
> ISAIAH 55:1-2

What have you pursued in your life in hopes that it would provide lasting satisfaction—relationships, money, success, status, possessions? Explain.

What do you long for most right now? How have you been pursuing it?

How would your life be different if you truly believed you have everything you need? How would this belief affect your relationships? Your work? Your service to others?

What do you need to surrender to the Lord right now in order to allow his blessings, peace, and joy to go deeper into your heart?

Take a few minutes to ask God to reveal anything that you have been chasing that is taking your focus off of him. Surrender anything that he brings to mind. Close by spending a few additional minutes in prayer, praising him for providing his true rest and contentment for your soul.

DEEPER

Jesus has not only liberated us from the Enemy but also invited us to join the fight. As C. S. Lewis explained, "Christianity is the story of how the rightful king has landed, you might say landed in disguise, and is calling us all to take part in his great campaign of sabotage."[2] It can feel like we are in a war *because we are in one.* Yet it is a war in which our King has won the decisive victory—and because he has been victorious, we can be too.

I know many people who are so discouraged by their continuous fumbles and failures that they've begun to doubt that God has changed their lives. Maybe you feel like that. But what if I told you that your struggles, rather than being a sign of something wrong with you, are actually a sign of something right?

Picture a battlefield in the midst of the heat of a firefight. Amid the chaos of bombs detonating and bullets flying, there are two kinds of people on the field. The first looks calm and still, unaffected by the destruction. The second appears agitated, clearly fighting a war within—battling fear, doubt, anxiety, terror—as the war wages without. What makes the two soldiers different? The first person appears peaceful because he is *dead.* The second person is aware of the battle because they are alive. It is the same spiritually.

The spiritually dead do not struggle with sin. Your struggles, far from being a sign of your spiritual death, may be one of your greatest assurances that you are alive. You have not been freed from your struggle against sin. You have been freed to struggle. Now you must learn how to struggle well, for you have a real fight on your hands.

— FROM CHAPTER 2 OF REST & WAR

How do you tend to view your "continuous fumbles and failures" in life?

How does it help you to know that your struggles, far from being a sign of your spiritual death, is actually an assurance that you are spiritually alive?

What is one way that you will "struggle well" this week?

For Next Week: Before your group's next session, read or review chapters 3 and 4 in *Rest & War*. Pay special attention to what each chapter has to say about surveying the battlefield.

NOTES

1. Ben Sherwood, *The Survivor's Club: The Secrets and Science That Could Save Your Life* (New York: Grand Central Publishing, 2009).
2. C. S. Lewis, *Mere Christianity* (1952; reprint, New York: HarperCollins, 1980), 45.

RHYTHMS OF A WELL-FOUGHT LIFE

REST
& WAR

AUTHORED BY BEN STUART

SESSION TWO

AWAY AND TOWARD

Do not be conformed to this world, but be transformed by the renewal of your mind, that by testing you may discern what is the will of God, what is good and acceptable and perfect.

ROMANS 12:2 ESV

WELCOME

Last summer, a collection of volunteers from our church and a local community center gathered on a little strip of grass next to a historic church in Washington, DC. In the center of the city, this neglected plot of ground had grown a tangle of weeds and collected all manner of garbage. On a single day, this team went to work clearing the grounds of trash and weeds. The old was cast out. Then they built planter boxes, filled them with nutrient-rich soil, and sowed them with seeds. In the span of a few hours, beauty replaced brokenness, vines were planted where garbage once rotted, and new life budded where previously no life was found.

Yet even though the plot of ground had been transformed in a moment, the work was not done. Counselors needed to guide kids from the community center in the work of tending the garden. For fruit to flourish, this new garden needed willing hands to engage in the constant work of renewal. Weeds had to be pulled, and plants needed to be watered. Garbage had be be removed and good soil tilled. And as these students have tended their garden, they have experienced the thrill of seeing the fruit of their labor rise up and flourish.

The same principle applies to the Christian life. Our complete renovation happened in a moment. When Jesus went to work on us, he brought life where there was once only death, beauty where there was once only ashes, and planted within us the possibility of growth. We were justified—made right with God—in a moment. Now our Counselor, the Holy Spirit, guides us in the work of sanctification: uprooting old ways of thinking and living, and cultivating new desires and new decisions.

Yet the "weeds" of old habits, old struggles, and old addictions still rise up in the soil of our soul. So, the new insights and inclinations the Lord planted deep within us must be cultivated and tended daily to reach their full potential. Though at times we can feel wearied by the necessity of this constant work, we can find hope in knowing it is not in vain. God has turned our garbage into a garden, and our work of cultivating right thinking and right living can produce much good for ourselves and for those around us.

SHARE

Before we jump into today's session, take a few minutes to introduce yourself to anyone you didn't meet during the first session and share any highlights that you have from last week's personal study. Then, to get things started, discuss one of the following questions

> ➤ As you look back at your life, what are some old ways of thinking and living that you have seen God uproot from your life? Conversely, what are some new desires and perspectives you have seen him plant?

— *or* —

> ➤ As you look at your life, consider what aspects of the garden of your soul need tending. Has some "garbage" thinking blown back in? Are the weeds of some bad habits peeking back through the soil? Are there some good habits that need intentional tending?

READ

Invite someone to read aloud the following passage. Listen for fresh insights as you hear the verses being read and then discuss the questions that follow.

> *If then you have been raised with Christ, seek the things that are above, where Christ is, seated at the right hand of God. Set your minds on things that are above, not on things that are on earth. For you have died, and your life is hidden with Christ in God. When Christ who is your life appears, then you also will appear with him in glory.*
>
> *Put to death therefore what is earthly in you: sexual immorality, impurity, passion, evil desire, and covetousness,*

which is idolatry. On account of these the wrath of God is coming. In these you too once walked, when you were living in them. But now you must put them all away: anger, wrath, malice, slander, and obscene talk from your mouth. Do not lie to one another, seeing that you have put off the old self with its practices and have put on the new self, which is being renewed in knowledge after the image of its creator. Here there is not Greek and Jew, circumcised and uncircumcised, barbarian, Scythian, slave, free; but Christ is all, and in all.

Put on then, as God's chosen ones, holy and beloved, compassionate hearts, kindness, humility, meekness, and patience, bearing with one another and, if one has a complaint against another, forgiving each other; as the Lord has forgiven you, so you also must forgive. And above all these put on love, which binds everything together in perfect harmony. And let the peace of Christ rule in your hearts, to which indeed you were called in one body. And be thankful. Let the word of Christ dwell in you richly, teaching and admonishing one another in all wisdom, singing psalms and hymns and spiritual songs, with thankfulness in your hearts to God. And whatever you do, in word or deed, do everything in the name of the Lord Jesus, giving thanks to God the Father through him.

COLOSSIANS 2:1-17 ESV

Paul urges the Colossians to "put away" certain activities and "put on" a new set of attributes. Read through the passage and note the motivations he gives them for doing so. What are some of the ways of living that he encourages them to abandon?

According to this passage, what are some of the ways of operating that Paul champions?

WATCH

Play the video segment for session two (use the streaming video access provided on the inside front cover). As you watch, use the following outline to record any thoughts or concepts that stand out to you.

We must survey the battlefield and assess our situation before we can implement a successful strategy for overcoming the Enemy. The Christian life involves eliminating threats, fighting for freedom, and bringing peace where before there had only been chaos.

Many of us realize the spiritual life is difficult. We get discouraged by our situation and wonder why we can't break free of certain habits and addictions. But we must remember the Bible is filled with words like *war* and *fight* and *struggle*. We need a strategy for victory.

The spiritual life is one movement with two parts. It is a movement *away* from things that promote isolation from God. It is a movement *toward* things that promote intimacy with God.

Theologians called this overall process *sanctification*—the act of setting something apart as holy unto God.

The act of moving *away* from sinful ways of thinking and living is called *mortification*. We put to death our former ways that impeded our intimacy with God.

The act of moving *toward* godly ways of thinking and living is called *vivification*. We cultivate new ways of living that we want to thrive and flourish.

God is always with us, but the quality of our relationship requires us to spend time with him, study his Word, learn his ways, and cultivate intimacy. Drawing closer to him also requires us to move away from decisions that impede our devotion to him.

We cannot judge the spiritual condition of others based on snapshot moments. Peter and Judas both denied Christ, but they made different choices about how they faced the consequences of their betrayal. We never know what God is doing in a human life at any given moment.

How can we know the Spirit of God is working within us? We begin to hate what we used to love and love what we used to hate. Although we still struggle and stumble, we are able to pull back the lens and see progress over time.

So, rather than be discouraged by our struggles, we should recognize that sanctification takes time and requires us to experience the ups and downs of life. Our struggles should not cause us to doubt God's presence and power but affirm the way that he is working in us.

If we want to grow, we must assess the battlefield and where we are in regard to it. We have to have the courage to ask God what he wants to uproot in our lives and what he wants to plant. We have to learn how to cultivate intimacy with God so that it might flourish.

DISCUSS

Take a few minutes within your group to discuss the message and explore these concepts in Scripture.

1. When have you recently been discouraged because of your struggles? How did you handle your discouragement?

2. When you first became a Christian, did you think your life would become easier or harder? How have your expectations changed since that time?

3. How would you define the process of *sanctification* to someone who was unfamiliar with this term and the Christian faith? What has shaped your definition?

4. What are some things you are *mortifying* (putting to death) as you follow Christ? What are some things you are *vivifying* (bringing to life) as you grow in Christ?

5. What are the dangers in judging someone else's spiritual condition based on a snapshot moment or first impression? When has someone judged you in that way?

6. On the battlefield, only the soldiers who are actually alive are aware of the struggle raging around them. In the Christian life, only those who are spiritually alive are aware of the struggles around them. How does this give you hope?

RESPOND

In this session, you explored the process of *sanctification* and what it means to put certain ways of living to death so other ways of living can thrive. Today, think of at least one thing that God wants you to put to death (a relationship, old habit, negative attitude, addiction). Next, think of at least one thing that God wants you to cultivate and bring to life (spending time in prayer, studying the Bible, serving others, and the like). After you have listed these, spend a few minutes developing your strategies to both move away from things you want to uproot and toward the things you want to cultivate. Once again, no one will see your responses unless you choose to share them.

STEP 1: MORTIFY

What God wants you to uproot, move away from,
and put to death:

-
-
-
-
-

Strategies for moving away from these things in your life:

-
-
-
-
-

STEP 2: VIVIFY

What God wants you to plant, move toward, and cultivate:

-
-
-
-
-

Strategies for moving toward these things in your life:

-
-
-
-
-

Review your answers and ask God to meet you where you are at this time.

PRAY

Conclude your session by sharing any requests you would like the group to lift up in prayer. Thank God for the ways that he is working and moving in each person's life right now. Ask him for strength, patience, and hope to continue pushing through your struggles and growing in your faith. Praise him for winning the war and giving you the soul rest that you crave.

PERSONAL STUDY

Continue exploring the concepts that you discussed during this week's group meeting by engaging in the following exercises for your personal study time. Be sure to write down any key points that stand out to you so you can share at the next meeting.

CONNECT

Check in with your group members during the upcoming week and continue the discussion you had with them at your last gathering. Grab coffee or dinner or reach out by text and share what's going on in your heart. Use the following questions to help guide your conversation.

Think back on what you have read in *Rest & War* and learned during the past two sessions. At this stage in your journey, what key truths and concepts have stood out to you as you have sought to resist the Enemy's strategy and develop greater intimacy with God?

How do you feel when you look at your life and "survey the battlefield"? In which areas do you need more strength and power to experience victory through God's Spirit?

How has the group helped you in this effort to this point? Does it help knowing that others are wrestling with similar issues and battles as you? Why or why not?

REFLECT

When I was in college, I lived one summer at a church in the center of downtown Denver, Colorado. The church had purchased an old grocery store and transformed it into a house of worship and a community center that provided all manner of material, emotional, and spiritual support for the community. In time, I learned from a member of the church that the grocery store had abandoned the area years before because of the high crime in the neighborhood. This church member, who had come to faith in Jesus through the ministry of the church, laughed as he told me, "Before I knew Christ, I used to rob this store. Now I work here every week to serve the community." His testimony reminds me of verse 28 of Ephesians 4. Read the passage below a few times and then answer the questions that follow.

Now this I say and testify in the Lord, that you must no longer walk as the Gentiles do, in the futility of their minds. They are darkened in their understanding, alienated from the life of God because of the ignorance that is in them, due to their hardness of heart. They have become callous and have given themselves up to sensuality, greedy to practice every kind of impurity. But that is not the way you learned Christ!—assuming that you have heard about him and were taught in him, as the truth is in Jesus, to put off your old self, which belongs to your former manner of life and is corrupt through deceitful desires, and to be renewed in the spirit of your minds, and to put on the new self, created after the likeness of God in true righteousness and holiness

Therefore, having put away falsehood, let each one of you speak the truth with his neighbor, for we are members one of another. Be angry and do not sin; do not let the sun go down on your anger, and give no opportunity to the devil. Let the thief no longer steal, but rather let him labor, doing honest work with his own hands, so that he may have something to share with anyone in need. Let no corrupting talk come out of your mouths, but only such as is good for building up, as fits the occasion, that it may give grace to those who hear. And do not grieve the Holy Spirit of God, by whom you were sealed for the day of redemption. Let all bitterness and wrath and anger and clamor and slander be put away from you, along with all malice. Be kind to one another, tenderhearted, forgiving one another, as God in Christ forgave you.

Therefore be imitators of God, as beloved children. And walk in love, as Christ loved us and gave himself up for us, a fragrant offering and sacrifice to God.

EPHESIANS 4:17–5:2 ESV

Paul points out that the Gentiles—people from various nations who do not know God—are separated from his life because of their lack of information ("ignorance" in verse 18) about God and a lack of inclination to seek him ("hardness of heart" in verse 18)! Does this resonate with your experience before coming to know Jesus? Have you seen this to be true in your life or in the lives of some of your loved ones?

As believers in Jesus, we did not create our "new self" (verse 24). Rather, our new life in God was "created" (verse 24) by the grace of God when we learned and received the truth about Jesus (see verses 20–21) and were sealed with his very Spirit (see verse 30). Can you recall when this happened to you? What made you interested in learning about Jesus? What made you desire to know Him? Who helped you in that journey?

In this passage, Paul uses the imagery of changing our clothing. The early church used to enact this imagery at baptism. They would take off their old clothes before being baptized and put on new robes afterward to symbolize this radical break from their "old self" and embracing of their "new self." Make a list of the qualities of the old life that Paul encourages us to disrobe. Do any of these still trouble you? Which ones are difficult for you to cast off?

Now make a list of the ways of living that he encourages believers to put on. Which one stands out to you as something you would like to see more of in your life? Write a few sentences about how your relationships might change if you put on that way of living. Consider writing out a prayer asking God for help putting this new way of living on.

Finally, notice the communal nature of these commands! So much of the fruit of our new relationship with Jesus manifests itself in our relationships with one another. How might your community of faith look different if together you walked out these commands together (see 4:17; 5:2)? Try to picture in your mind what that might look like. How could you encourage one another in that journey?

WORSHIP

The great saint Augustine wrote in *Confessions*, "Command what you will, and give me what you command!"[1] He understood that we need the Spirit of God to empower us to live truly spiritual lives. Later in Ephesians, Paul calls his audience to be "filled with the Spirit," and then, with five participles (verbs that "participate" in that main command to "be filled"), he tells us what that life looks like:

> And do not get drunk with wine, for that is debauchery, but be filled with the Spirit, addressing one another in psalms and hymns and spiritual songs, singing and making melody to the Lord with your heart, giving thanks always and for everything to God the Father in the name of our Lord Jesus Christ, submitting to one another out of reverence for Christ.
>
> EPHESIANS 5:18–21 ESV

Write out the participles in the passage above that fill out what it means to live filled with the Spirit of God. (Helpful hint: participles typically end in -*ing*!)

A friend of mine often says, "Worship is a weapon." Singing in our hearts and with our people often proves to be one of our greatest strategies to overcome discouragement, temptation, or lack of motivation. Do you have a psalm or hymn or worship song that helps you? Is there a verse or line that helps stir up your affections for the Lord? Consider writing it out below.

Gratitude can also serve as a powerful antidote to grumbling. List three to five things below for which you are truly grateful.

Are there some people who have helped you find strength and hope in your journey with God? Jot down a quick note of encouragement to them. It can be as simple as, "You came to mind today and I thanked God for you." Consider sending it to them, and see how that impacts your attitude and their day!

DEEPER

When I was in elementary school, with a little help from my brother and his friends, I was elected chief of the fire patrol at my elementary school. That meant that if a fire drill was conducted, I had certain responsibilities to fulfill to ensure the safety of other students. Responsibilities like timing the length of the drill with the assistant principal's stopwatch.

About a month into the school year, the alarm went off. I was sitting in class and our teacher said, "Students, get in line and walk toward the back of the school." I was a student, so I got in line and filed out like everybody else. I walked about midway down the hall when it hit me: *Wait a minute, I'm the fire chief. I shouldn't be going this way. The stopwatch is in the desk in the assistant principal's office at the front of the school!*

Panic struck my heart. But after a few seconds, the crisis was resolved when I remembered the day the principal appointed me fire chief. The highest authority in the school had given me a new identity that held more weight than that of "student." I stepped out of line. As eyes around me widened in terror, I began to run the opposite direction. Feeling the stares of my entire class, I cried out as I sprinted, "I am the fire chief!"

We need to charge forward with our new identity and mission. Jesus declared war on the chaos of sin in order to bring us into the peace of his kingdom. The new identity he has given us comes with a whole new set of activities. We run a different way now. Our king has commissioned us to join him in the work of making war and cultivating rest.

— FROM CHAPTER 3 OF *REST & WAR*

What are some of the responsibilities that you have as a disciple of Christ?

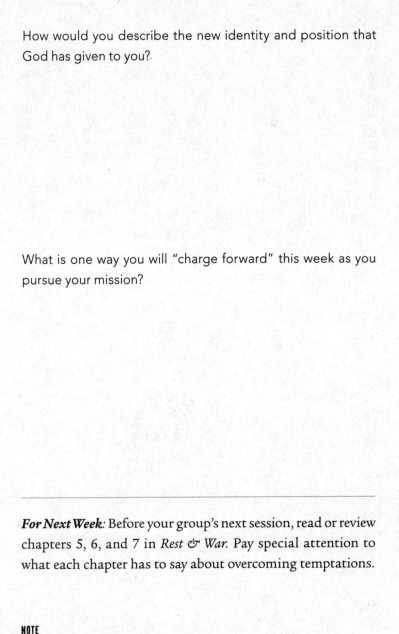

How would you describe the new identity and position that God has given to you?

What is one way you will "charge forward" this week as you pursue your mission?

For Next Week: Before your group's next session, read or review chapters 5, 6, and 7 in *Rest & War.* Pay special attention to what each chapter has to say about overcoming temptations.

NOTE

1. Saint Augustine of Hippo, *Confessions* (AD 397–400), book 10, chapter 29.

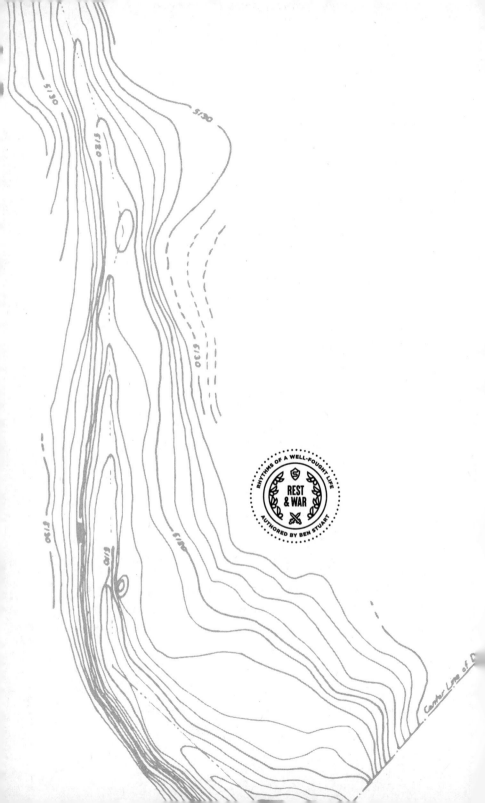

RHYTHMS OF A WELL-FOUGHT LIFE

REST
& WAR

AUTHORED BY BEN STUART

SESSION THREE

DOWNSTREAM AND UPSTREAM

Watch and pray so that you will not fall into temptation.
The spirit is willing, but the flesh is weak.

MATTHEW 26:41

WELCOME

My least favorite lecture in marketing class shaped my life more than any other moment in college. On that day, our professor endeavored to train a room full of budding marketing majors to employ a potent strategy for accomplishing our goal of selling a product. He pulled the curtain back on how we are marketed to, and I have never seen the world the same again.

He first explained that we do not spend our time or energy studying the product in question. Nor do we aim our creativity at explaining to our target audience the virtues or qualities of our particular commodity. Rather, we focus our energy on studying the people who we want to convince to give us their money. Specifically, we contemplate their insecurities. We then consider how to highlight those perceived deficiencies. Pick at their insecurities. Raise their anxieties to as high a pitch as possible. After we heighten their dissatisfaction through repeated messaging, we then present our product as the remedy for the discomfort that we aggravated. We irritate to influence so they will do what we want and give us what is theirs.

I resolved that day that I did not want to work in marketing. Now, I realize that not all advertisers do this. Some people enter this field with much purer motives than my cynical ones cited above. But I see this influence all around me now. You and I are surrounded by messages designed to influence our behavior in order to give someone else what they want—not necessarily to provide us with what we need.

Friend, that is how the Devil works on us too. He understands these basic concepts I learned that day in class. What we think about will determine what we care about. And what we care about, we will chase. So, as we contemplate the struggles and strategies of the spiritual life, we must be aware of the propaganda campaign of the Enemy so we can actively choose who influences our thinking, our loving, and our living.

SHARE

Before we jump into today's session, take a few minutes to share any insights you have from last week's personal study. Then, to get things started, discuss one of the following questions:

➤ Have you seen the marketing tactic described above play out in your life or in the lives of your friends? Can you think of an example?

— or —

➤ How have you seen this same pattern (deception
fuels temptation, which leads to destruction) spiritually? Have you seen this in your own life? Can you
share an example?

READ

Invite someone to read aloud the following passage. Listen for
fresh insights as you hear the verse being read and then discuss the questions that follow.

*Then Jesus was led by the Spirit into the wilderness to be
tempted by the devil. After fasting forty days and forty
nights, he was hungry. The tempter came to him and said,
"If you are the Son of God, tell these stones to become bread."*

*Jesus answered, "It is written: 'Man shall not live on
bread alone, but on every word that comes from the mouth
of God.'"*

*Then the devil took him to the holy city and had him
stand on the highest point of the temple. "If you are the Son
of God," he said, "throw yourself down. For it is written:*

*"'He will command his angels concerning you,
   and they will lift you up in their hands,
      so that you will not strike your foot against a stone.'"*
*Jesus answered him, "It is also written: 'Do not put the
Lord your God to the test.'"*

*Again, the devil took him to a very high mountain and
showed him all the kingdoms of the world and their splendor.*

"All this I will give you," he said, *"if you will bow down and worship me."*

Jesus said to him, "Away from me, Satan! For it is written: 'Worship the Lord your God, and serve him only.'"

Then the devil left him, and angels came and attended him.

MATTHEW 4:1–11

Notice how the Devil starts the conversation. He comes when Jesus is weak (and hopefully more susceptible), but he does not start the conversation by discussing physical hunger or the virtues of bread. How does he begin his marketing strategy? Why do you think it was important for him to begin by questioning whether or not Jesus was really the loved Son of a caring Father? How would that have potentially influenced Jesus' behavior?

When has the Enemy recently tried to tempt you during a weak or vulnerable moment? How did he tailor his temptations to your specific weaknesses at that time?

WATCH

Play the video segment for session three. Use the following outline of main points as you watch to jot down your thoughts, questions, or anything that stands out to you.

In Jesus' life, the wilderness was a place where he overcame temptations and cultivated devotion with his Father. In our wilderness experiences, learning how to identify and overcome temptations is also crucial to our spiritual growth and maturity.

Even Jesus, the Son of God, was not exempt from temptation during his time on earth. If temptation came for Christ, it will be coming for us as well. In fact, temptation may come into our lives in even greater amounts than it did before our conversion.

Satan tempted Jesus when he was the most vulnerable—when he was hungry and weary from his fast. He targets us the same way—when we're at our weakest in some area of life.

Every trial triggers a temptation. When we are hungry, or angry, or lonely, a voice of sweet release will come offering an escape. It will usually alleviate the pain in the moment. But it will also come with a cost that we really won't want to pay.

In order to overcome temptations, we must know our weaknesses and recognize how the Enemy will target those areas. Like a master strategist, the devil has studied the patterns of behavior in our lives, the ways we think and act, and our preferences and proclivities.

If we want to overcome temptation, we need to recognize the Enemy will try to make it look attractive to us. The Bible provides four ways for us to respond when he does this:

Eliminate the moment: If we know that temptation always leads to sin, then we need to avoid those situations where the Enemy could set a trap for us. We become architects of our environments and avoid cues that kickstart our cravings.

Look downstream: When temptation comes, we need to pause and consider what will be the outcome of our decision to act. Is it an outcome that we want? If we don't like our outputs, then we need to consider our inputs.

Look upstream: When temptation comes, we need to consider what is causing us to want to engage in it. The Enemy will build an environment where we are primed for a fall. We have to strike at the root of the sin before it begins to produce fruit.

Have a good offense: The best way for us to resist the lure of the devil is to have a healthy, thriving, and intimate relationship with God.

Take a moment to consider how the Enemy is getting to you. Be a student of yourself. Forsake the deceptive streams and enjoy the inexhaustible fountain of living water in your Father.

DISCUSS

Take a few minutes within your group to discuss the message and explore these concepts in Scripture.

1. Not even Jesus, the Son of God, was exempt from temptation. What does this say about temptation in your life? What strategies does Jesus provide for battling temptation?

2. Think about a time when you have been tempted during moments of weakness, vulnerability, or fatigue. How did the Enemy's attacks appeal to what you felt you needed at that moment?

3. Do you agree that every trial naturally includes temptations for escape, comfort, and pleasure? Why or why not?

4. How can expecting to be tempted during a trial help you prepare in advance?

5. Think about an area of weakness that causes you struggles and temptations. What have you learned about yourself from fighting this particular spiritual battle?

6. How have you altered your environment to remove or reduce cues that kickstart your cravings? How has this helped you overcome certain temptations?

RESPOND

Take a few minutes after your group discussion time to explore the four-part strategy for resisting temptation that was outlined in this week's teaching. Begin by choosing a temptation that you consistently find hard to resist. Once again, no one else will see what you write below, so choose a temptation that you actually want to overcome. Next, respond to each of the following questions to help you develop spiritual defenses for this particular temptation.

Strategy 1: Eliminate the moment. What are some ways that you can change your environment to eliminate cues that lead to this temptation?

Strategy 2: Look upstream. What greater need, longing, desire, or deficit do you think this temptation is attempting to address in your life?

Strategy 3: Look downstream. Based on past experience, what is the short-term result and long-term impact of giving in to this temptation?

Strategy 4: Have a good offense. What is one truth or promise from Scripture that you can claim when you encounter this temptation?

PRAY

Conclude your session by sharing any requests you would like the group to lift up in prayer, especially as it relates to the exercise you have just completed. As you pray for each other, ask God to protect you and empower you to overcome the Enemy's temptations and deceptions. Thank the Lord for the progress you have made and for his help in making you grow stronger in your faith. Praise him also for the gift of his Son, Jesus, who willingly went to the cross to pay the price for your sins so that you can share in the victory that he has won.

PERSONAL STUDY

Continue exploring the concepts that you discussed during this week's group meeting by engaging in the following exercises for your personal study time. Be sure to write down any key points that stand out to you so you can share at the next meeting.

CONNECT

Check in with your group members during the upcoming week and continue the discussion you had with them at your last gathering. Grab coffee or dinner or reach out by text and share what's going on in your heart. Use the following questions to help guide your conversation.

What key point stood out to you from your last group's meeting? Why do you think that particular point is so significant to you at this particular time?

Has the way you consider temptations in your life changed since reading *Rest & War* and starting this group? Why or why not?

What are some ongoing temptations that you know you need help resisting? How can others in your group help you?

REFLECT

If you are unsettled by what's been covered during this week's teaching, or if you are struggling more intensely with certain temptations, remember to take it as a sign of growth. If you're gaining new insights and strategies on how to resist temptation and to grow closer to God, the Enemy may be assaulting you with unexpected and extra-intense temptations. As James points out below, this comes with the territory. To reinforce all you're absorbing about how temptations work, read through the following passage and answer the questions that follow.

> *Consider it pure joy, my brothers and sisters, whenever you face trials of many kinds, because you know that the testing of your faith produces perseverance. Let perseverance finish its work so that you may be mature and complete, not lacking anything. If any of you lacks wisdom, you should ask*

God, who gives generously to all without finding fault, and it will be given to you. But when you ask, you must believe and not doubt, because the one who doubts is like a wave of the sea, blown and tossed by the wind. That person should not expect to receive anything from the Lord. Such a person is double-minded and unstable in all they do.

When tempted, no one should say, "God is tempting me." For God cannot be tempted by evil, nor does he tempt anyone; but each person is tempted when they are dragged away by their own evil desire and enticed. Then, after desire has conceived, it gives birth to sin; and sin, when it is full-grown, gives birth to death.

JAMES 1:2–8, 13–15

Why does James say that you can take joy in facing trials of many kinds? What have you learned—about yourself, God, and the ways of the Enemy—from those trials?

Which particular sinful desires have resulted in the most painful consequences in your life? How do they influence your view of temptations presently?

What wisdom do you currently need to ask God to give you? How will this wisdom assist you in overcoming temptations?

WORSHIP

Talking about our sins, struggles, and shortcomings can be difficult, because shame often rises up and floods our minds. We can feel embarrassed by our desires, humiliated by our repeated failures, and tempted to believe that we are broken beyond repair. Yet this is also a tactic of the Enemy. Shame impedes strategic thinking, and often when we allow ourselves to be buried by feelings of worthlessness, we inhibit the helpful work of analyzing what we did so we can make necessary changes.

The writer of Hebrews helps us here. I love that in the text below, he calls his original audience to *more*. As he addresses their struggle against sin in verse 4, he says of their attempts, "You aren't even bleeding yet!" They could fight much harder than they were fighting now. Yet even as he points this out, there is no shame. Notice the motivations that surround that exhortation. Particularly, notice how he describes their relationship with their God.

Consider him who endured from sinners such hostility against himself, so that you may not grow weary or fainthearted. In your struggle against sin you have not yet resisted to the point of shedding your blood. And have you forgotten the exhortation that addresses you as sons

> *"My son, do not regard lightly the discipline of the Lord;*
> *nor be weary when reproved by him.*
> *For the Lord disciplines the one he loves,*
> *and chastises every son whom he receives."*

It is for discipline that you have to endure. God is treating you as sons. For what son is there whom his father does not discipline? If you are left without discipline, in which all have participated, then you are illegitimate children and not sons. Besides this, we have had earthly fathers who disciplined us and we respected them. Shall we not much more be subject to the Father of spirits and live? For they disciplined us for a short time as it seemed best to them, but he disciplines us for our good, that we may share his holiness. For the moment all discipline seems painful rather than pleasant, but later it yields the peaceful fruit of righteousness to those who have been trained by it.

Therefore lift your drooping hands and strengthen your weak knees, and make straight paths for your feet, so that what is lame may not be put out of joint but rather be healed.

HEBREWS 12:3–13 ESV

Six times, the author of Hebrews refers to his readers as "sons." You are a son (or daughter) who is dearly loved by your Father. Do not let the voice of shame in your mind try to convince you that you are anything less. So, why does your Father let you struggle with the remnants of sin's once proud reign?

Like a coach developing his players, he understands that the struggle will make you strong. It is discipline that develops.

When you struggle with temptation, are you tempted to believe that God does not love you? Do you believe you live under the frown of heaven? How does that perspective impact your motivation to engage in the process of sanctification?

How would your personal engagement in your struggle against sin change if you believed God was a coach training you rather than a judge condemning you?

What are some good qualities in your life that, with the benefit of hindsight, you see now were developed through difficult times in your life?

What do you think God is trying to teach you through your current struggles?

DEEPER

Years ago when I read Sun Tzu's *The Art of War*, I was surprised how little the author wrote about the actual moment of battle. Much of his attention focused on positioning troops in advantageous environments and avoiding compromising ones. The book is filled with lines like, "When in difficult country, do not encamp," and, "Do not linger in dangerously isolated positions."[1] He knew that success depends largely on knowledge of your surroundings.

Many of our most disappointing actions could also be eliminated by intentionally designing our environment. Do you miss morning workouts because you are too tired? Research shows that screen time disrupts sleep time, so try removing all screens from your bedroom. Do you constantly lose time to social media while at work? Put your phone out of arm's reach. Do you mindlessly overeat? Get all the junk food out of your house.

Take a moment to consider the circumstances in which you consistently compromise. Where are you? When is it? Who are you with? Have you allowed yourself to linger in dangerously isolated positions? Ask yourself, *Are there places I should no longer go? Are there certain times of the day or the week when I am particularly vulnerable to certain temptations? How can I move myself to a more secure environment in those moments?*

Many of the people who check into rehab facilities for addictions find they can get and stay sober in that supportive environment. But if they return to the same house, neighborhood haunts, and friendship groups where they had previously acted out, they relapse. Their sobriety depends largely on altering their surroundings.

Think of how the same principles apply to you. Become mindful of where you move, when you move, and who you move with. Know that your context will shape your character.

— FROM CHAPTER 5 OF *REST & WAR*

What would it look like in your life to intentionally design your environment?

What temptations might you avoid if you eliminated certain things from your environment?

Where are you making compromises? What needs to change today in your habits?

For Next Week: Before your group's next session, read or review chapters 8, 9, and 10 in *Rest & War.* Pay special attention to what each chapter has to say about cultivating devotion with God.

NOTE
1. Sun Tzu, *The Art of War*, trans. Leonel Giles (Mineola, NY: Ixia Press, 2019), 61.

RHYTHMS OF A WELL-FOUGHT LIFE

REST & WAR

AUTHORED BY BEN STUART

SESSION FOUR

CONSISTENCY AND CREATIVITY

Pray in the Spirit on all occasions with all kinds of prayers
and requests. With this in mind, be alert and always keep on
praying for all the Lord's people.

EPHESIANS 6:18

WELCOME

We filmed the videos for this Bible study far out in the wilds
of west Texas for one compelling reason: *my sanity*. Yes, we
liked the beauty of the backdrop. Yes, we liked that it connected with all the passages of Scripture about the wilderness.

But the driving force behind that decision was that I needed to get out of town!

When life gets too busy for me, I have found that it helps to find a few days to exit into the desert. There is something about the stillness and quiet of the terrain that helps me still and quiet my soul before the Lord. The location was not just for you, my friend, it was for me! It's a place I go to rekindle the flame of my affection for Jesus.

The cultivation of intimacy with God requires consistency and creativity. And one of the creative ways I have found to deepen my devotion to the Lord is to get out into the wild places. You might think that sounds romantic and inspiring and want to try it for yourself. That's great. Or you may think solitude in the desert sounds like punishment. That's okay too. You don't have to go where I go. But you do need to ask, "What helps me cultivate intimacy with God?" Do you have an answer? It's important you do.

As it relates to consistency in our spiritual life, I don't think using the language of "spiritual discipline" is wrong. Yet in today's vernacular, "discipline" often brings up feelings of obligation rather than anticipation. And, if we are not careful, we can easily slip into the mentality that what God wants from us is the accomplishment of tasks in order to check off the right boxes so we can rise up and declare, "I am a disciplined person." But God calls us to something much more inspiring than this.

I never say to my wife, "I will now initiate the discipline of taking you out to dinner." That would be a bad way to start a date night. Now, making time to consistently be together does take effort: organizing our calendar, securing babysitters, researching restaurants, and so on. But these efforts are a means to an end, not an end to themselves. The end is also not to say, "I have done my duty as a husband." The disciplines exist to position myself to enjoy my relationship with the woman I have made a covenant with to love for a lifetime. It is duty with the aim of delight. Activity with the end goal of cultivating intimacy.

The same is true spiritually. Disciplines are the means to an end, never the end in themselves. This is another trick of the Enemy. If he can reduce the cultivation of intimacy with God to an obligation of duties, we are more likely to drop them over time. But if we understand sanctification as a cultivation of devotion with the Lord who made a covenant to love us, then we can pursue the enjoyment of that love with greater zeal. This is the end goal: consistently and creatively cultivating intimacy with the God in whose "right hand are pleasures forevermore" (Psalm 16:11 ESV).

SHARE

Before we jump into today's session, take a few minutes to share any insights that you have from last week's personal study. Then, to get things started, discuss one of the following questions:

> How would you say you are doing when it comes to *consistently* meeting with God? Is there room for improvement in this area?

— or —

> How would you say you are doing when it comes to *creatively* interacting with God? Are there practices you are following that seem stagnant?

READ

Invite someone to read aloud the following passage. Listen for fresh insights as you hear the verses being read and then discuss the questions that follow.

> *"Remain in me, as I also remain in you. No branch can bear fruit by itself; it must remain in the vine. Neither can you bear fruit unless you remain in me. I am the vine; you are the branches. If you remain in me and I in you, you will bear much fruit; apart from me you can do nothing. If you do not remain in me, you are like a branch that is thrown away and withers; such branches are picked up, thrown into the fire and burned. If you remain in me and my words remain in you, ask whatever you wish, and it will be done for you. This is to my Father's glory, that you bear much fruit, showing yourselves to be my disciples."*
>
> JOHN 15:4–8

Why does Jesus say that it is important for you to stay connected to him?

What promise does Jesus give to those who choose to remain in him?

WATCH

Play the video segment for session four (use the streaming video access provided on the inside front cover). As you watch, use the following outline to record any thoughts or concepts that stand out to you.

When God wanted to shape his saints—Abraham, Moses, the Israelites, David—he would meet them in desolate places where he could cultivate their devotion without distractions. The best way to dislodge temptation from your heart is to replace it by cultivating devotion with God.

The story of Hosea and Gomer illustrates our tendency to stray from God's love and seek out temporary pleasures. Gomer ran to the city to indulge in all it had to offer. Temptation offers much, but it takes more than it gives. When we think it will add, it subtracts.

So many of us, like Gomer, have gone to all kinds of wayward roads for satisfaction—and it's taken more than it's given. The beauty of the gospel is that God wants to allure us, and speak tenderly to us, and to call us to return to enjoy the love of the Father.

Our modern life is not conducive to the environment our soul needs to flourish in our relationship with God. So, we must go to war to find rest. While the Enemy tries to exploit our reliance on technology, we can actively determine to cultivate intimacy with God.

Jesus had three years to change the world, yet he never neglected the rhythm of moving into a city for intense ministry and then going out into the wilderness to cultivate intimacy with his Father. His example demonstrates the perfect balance of war and rest.

Jesus developed this rhythm in his life—of cultivating devotion with the Father—and we are to do the same. As we do this, we should think in terms of two categories:

Consistency: We need a consistent rhythm—a regular time, an undistracted place, and a specific plan—for cultivating intimacy with the Lord. When we daily load our minds with thoughts of God, it fuels the furnace of our affections and the engine of our actions.

Creativity: We need to find different ways to interact with God to keep our relationship fresh, vibrant, and dynamic. We must be willing to take risks, pursue God in new ways, act spontaneously, and relish the joy of being together with the Lord.

Some of us have been followers of Jesus for years but there's so much of his Word that has never entered our minds. Find a creative way to be consistent in your time with God.

Like Saint Augustine, when we surrender the pursuit of earthly pleasures and devote our hearts to knowing God, we experience freedom, joy, power for the battle and rest for our weary souls.

DISCUSS

Take a few minutes within your group to discuss the message and explore these concepts in Scripture.

1. What does "cultivating devotion with God" look like for you? When have you experienced this kind of pursuit with the Lord?

2. Are you vulnerable to turning to social media for validation, affirmation, or attention? How often do you rely on your phone when you're feeling lonely or bored?

3. What stands out or resonates the most with you in the story of Hosea and Gomer? Why do you find this so significant or striking?

4. How would you describe the spiritual rhythm you presently have in your relationship with God?

5. Do you agree that consistency is essential in order to cultivate devotion in your relationship with God? What are some ways you can be more consistent?

6. Do you also agree that creativity is essential to cultivating devotion in your relationship with God? How can you be more creative?

RESPOND

Take a few minutes after your group discussion time to explore the two aspects of spending time with God that were outlined in this week's teaching. First, look at ways that you can be more intentional about setting a time, place, and plan for interacting with God each day. Next, evaluate some strategies for becoming more creative in your time with him. Use the following questions to guide you in building this strategy for developing intimacy with God.

STEP 1: CONSISTENCY

When is a time you could consistently meet with God each day?

Where is a place you could consistently meet with God without distractions?

What plan will you put in place to make sure you stick to this strategy?

STEP 2: CREATIVITY

Which of the following options would you be willing to try this week?

➤ Get out somewhere in nature and thank God for his creation.

➤ Listen to a worship song and spend time just praising God.

➤ Explore some historical church traditions (such as baptism, fasting, or communion) to better understand their significance and how they have brought people closer to God over the centuries.

➤ Read a passage of Scripture and talk with God out loud about what it means to you.

➤ Surprise a neighbor or friend with a meal or do some other act of service.

➤ Write your thoughts in a journal and ask God to speak to you.

If none of these appeal to you, what *is* one out-of-the-box way you would be willing to be more creative in your daily interaction with God this next week?

PRAY

Conclude your session by sharing any requests you would like the group to lift up in prayer, including any related to the exercise you just completed. As you pray for each other, ask God to help you be more consistent in your prayer times and more open to looking for creative ways to interact with him. Ask for his continued protection and guidance in resisting the Enemy's strategies. Thank him for how he is revealing himself to each member in the group.

PERSONAL STUDY

Continue exploring the concepts that you discussed during this week's group meeting by engaging in the following exercises for your personal study time. Be sure to write down any key points that stand out to you so you can share at the next meeting.

CONNECT

Check in with your group members during the upcoming week and continue the discussion you had with them at your last gathering. Grab coffee or dinner or reach out by text and share what's going on in your heart. Use the following questions to help guide your conversation.

What struggles do you have when it comes to spending time with God each day?

How has investing more time in your relationship with God helped in the past to overcome temptations? What are some ways that you want to draw closer to God?

How can you help others in your group be accountable to the commitments that they made as it relates to spending time with God? How can the group help keep you accountable?

REFLECT

Sit for a few moments in silence, unplugged and undisturbed, and still your heart before God. Ask the Holy Spirit to empower and equip you as you consider how to cultivate devotion and draw closer to God. Keep in mind the example that Jesus set for his followers. When ministry and relationships drained him emotionally, spiritually, and physically, Jesus knew that he needed time alone with his Father to rest, recharge, and renew his energy. As you consider how you can establish a more rhythmic balance between the demands of battle and the need for rest, reflect on the following passage, using the questions that follow to guide you.

> As soon as they left the synagogue, they went with James and John to the home of Simon and Andrew. Simon's mother-in-law was in bed with a fever, and they immediately told Jesus about her. So he went to her, took her hand and helped her up. The fever left her and she began to wait on them.
>
> That evening after sunset the people brought to Jesus all the sick and demon-possessed. The whole town gathered at the door, and Jesus healed many who had various diseases. He also drove out many demons, but he would not let the demons speak because they knew who he was.
>
> Very early in the morning, while it was still dark, Jesus got up, left the house and went off to a solitary place, where he prayed.
>
> MARK 1:29-35

How do you think Jesus felt in light of the intense demands of ministering to so many people? How would you have felt in his place if you were doing this kind of service?

Mark states that Simon's mother-in-law was one of the people Jesus healed. How does the personal nature of this healing compare to Christ's interaction with virtually the whole town?

What demands and responsibilities in your life presently drain you the most? How do you recover and replenish in order to sustain your service to others?

What stands out to you about the fact that Jesus got up before sunrise and went to a solitary place to pray? How does his example influence the way you spend time with God?

WORSHIP

One of the strategies the Enemy likes to employ is to bring distractions and competing priorities into your life that will interrupt your prayer times. This is why it is important to not only have a *time* and *place* but also a *plan* for how you will spend your time each day with God. Throughout the Gospels, we find Jesus providing instructions to his disciples on how they should plan their prayer time and what their attitude should be when they approach their Heavenly Father. Read through these instructions that Jesus provides and answer the questions that follow.

> *"And when you pray, do not be like the hypocrites, for they love to pray standing in the synagogues and on the street corners to be seen by others. Truly I tell you, they have received their reward in full. But when you pray, go into your room, close the door and pray to your Father, who is unseen. Then your Father, who sees what is done in secret, will reward you. And when you pray, do not keep on babbling like pagans, for they think they will be heard because of their many words. Do not be like them, for your Father knows what you need before you ask him. This, then, is how you should pray:*
>
> > *"'Our Father in heaven,*
> > *hallowed be your name,*
> > *your kingdom come,*
> > *your will be done,*
> >   *on earth as it is in heaven.*
> > *Give us today our daily bread.*
> > *And forgive us our debts,*
> >   *as we also have forgiven our debtors.*

And lead us not into temptation,
but deliver us from the evil one.'

For if you forgive other people when they sin against
you, your heavenly Father will also forgive you. But if you
do not forgive others their sins, your Father will not forgive
your sins."

Matthew 6:5-14

Why do you think Jesus puts such an emphasis on the private and personal nature of prayer? What does he say about those who pray only to be seen by others?

The pagans of Jesus' day babbled on in their prayers in an attempt to impress their gods. What does Jesus say about this practice? What assurance do you have that God hears your prayers?

What word or phrase from the Lord's Prayer speaks directly to where you are spiritually right now? How can this awareness facilitate consistency in your prayer times this week?

Why do you think Jesus adds his warning about forgiving other people? What does this again reveal about the attitude of your heart that God is seeking when you pray?

DEEPER

When I ask people what it means to be *spiritual* or *godly* or *religious*, they often make a list of things a good spiritual person does and does not do. Spiritual people attend religious services, pray, meditate, read Scripture, and serve. They avoid going to certain places, saying certain things, and doing particular acts. They define spirituality as adhering to a list of dos and don'ts.

This version of spirituality guarantees one of two outcomes. First, you eventually get frustrated and ditch the list. Maybe you grew up under strict religious parents and in college you cast off your repressive restraints. Or maybe you joined a church out of a sincere desire to grow spiritually, but just couldn't seem to live up to the standard, and after a while you got tired of feeling like a failure. So you quit. The scenarios abound, but the short story is that the list got frustrating. So, you eventually forgot the whole thing.

Or second, and what I believe is far more dangerous, you've kept the list perfectly. You've obeyed all the rules. You've excelled at all the expectations. Now you look around at all the pathetic people who can't seem to get it together and you judge them. You pity them for their weakness, or you disdain them for their lack of discipline. You've been nurturing a smug self-righteousness because you are capable of something lesser mortals are not. And in your arrogance your heart has grown very cold.

Whether you are running from the rules or obsessing over them, *neither of these things is Christianity.* True spirituality is not adherence to a list of rules or activities. It is investment in the greatest of all relationships. While this cultivation involves doing activities, those activities are a means, not an end. And that makes all the difference.

— FROM CHAPTER 8 OF *REST & WAR*

How do you define what it means to be *spiritual, godly,* or *religious?*

When have you experienced the first outcome and become frustrated at your inability to live up to a list of impossible standards? How did God change this attitude in you?

When have you experienced the second outcome and started to look down on others because of their failure to keep the list perfectly? How did God change this attitude in you?

For Next Week: Before your group's next session, read or review chapters 11 and 12 in *Rest & War*. Pay special attention to what each chapter says about the importance of community.

RHYTHMS OF A WELL-FOUGHT LIFE

REST & WAR

AUTHORED BY BEN STUART

SESSION FIVE

FOCUS AND UNITY

Let us consider how we may spur one another on toward
love and good deeds, not giving up meeting together . . .
but encouraging one another.

HEBREWS 10:24

WELCOME

"When did you *ever* do anything by yourself?" I listened to an interview recently with a retired Navy SEAL. He was speaking specifically to other retired SEALS who might feel ashamed that they were struggling to succeed in their private lives after their time in the military was done. He discovered that many of them would beat themselves up for not being successful entrepeneurs in the private sector or leaders in their home, and they were chosing to bear the suffering of those shameful feelings in silence.

After proposing the above question, he continued by reminding them of their career as soldiers. They were trained by instructors, outfitted by weapons contractors, supplied vital information by the intelligence community, transported by other military personnel, and deployed along with their brothers in arms. All of their successes as soliders happened within, and because of, a supportive community. The man then encouraged them that continued success as husbands and leaders required the same communal support.

The same is true in our lives as followers of Christ. We need pastors, marriage counselors, business mentors, and encouraging friends in order to win in life. We all need each other in order to fully reach our potential. True of soldiers. True of leaders. True in families. And true spiritually. There is no shame in declaring that we need the support structure of a vital community. God rigged it that way. In fact, one of God's greatest gifts to us is, "us."

SHARE

Before we jump into today's session, take a few minutes to share any insights that you have from last week's personal study. Then, to get things started, discuss one of the following questions:

> ➤ Do you have areas in your life where you can clearly see the positive impact of a supportive community? If so, what are they?

— *or* —

> ➤ Do you find it easy or difficult to forge lasting friendships? Expand on your answer a bit.

READ

Invite someone to read aloud the following passage. Listen for fresh insights as you hear the verses being read and then discuss the questions that follow.

> *I thank my God every time I remember you. In all my prayers for all of you, I always pray with joy because of your partnership in the gospel from the first day until now, being confident of this, that he who began a good work in you will carry it on to completion until the day of Christ Jesus . . .*
>
> *Whatever happens, conduct yourselves in a manner worthy of the gospel of Christ. Then, whether I come and see you or only hear about you in my absence, I will know that you stand firm in the one Spirit, striving together as one for the faith of the gospel without being frightened in any way by those who oppose you. This is a sign to them that they will be destroyed, but that you will be saved—and that by God. For it has been granted to you on behalf of Christ not only to believe in him, but also to suffer for him, since you are going through the same struggle you saw I had, and now hear that I still have.*
>
> PHILIPPIANS 1:3–6, 27–30

What do you think Paul means when he advises you to "conduct yourself worthy of the gospel of Christ"? How does this manifest itself in your life on a daily basis?

Have you experienced a shared partnership with other believers to advance the gospel? If so, how did being part of that community strengthen your faith?

WATCH

Play the video segment for session four (use the streaming video access provided on the inside front cover). As you watch, use the following outline to record any thoughts or concepts that stand out to you.

The early church was like a highly focused band of warriors. They shared everything in common, devoted themselves to the apostles' teachings, and refused to let anything stop them. Cultures change when the community of faith has focus and unity.

Paul urged the Philippians to "conduct [themselves] in a manner worthy of the gospel of Christ" (Philippians 1:27). In the Greek, the phrase is the word *politeuesthe*, derived from *polis*, which means city. Paul reminded them that they were citizens of heaven and should act accordingly.

Paul wanted the members of the early church to stand firm in the faith, united by one spirit, and strive for the sake of the gospel message (see Philippians 3:20). Unity matters because when we live in a manner worthy of Jesus, we love the people he fought and died for.

True spirituality always works itself out in the context of community because one of God's greatest gifts to us is other people. He wants us to be united as the body of Christ.

We need each other to experience the healing that comes from confessing to one another. God is faithful to forgive our sins when we confess them to him (see 1 John 1:9). But if we want healing, we need to confess to other believers and pray for one another (see James 5:16).

We not only need connection to our Christian community for confession and healing, but we also need community because we share a mission to spread the gospel and advance God's kingdom. We accomplish these goals with greater impact *together* than apart.

God has scattered his gifts in the body of Christ so we need one another to accomplish greater things than we could achieve alone. God gave some to be apostles, some to be prophets, some to be teachers, and some to equip the saints for the works of service (see Ephesians 4:11–13).

The most effective way we can war and experience rest is through our community of brothers and sisters in Christ. True spirituality always works itself out in the context of community.

DISCUSS

Take a few minutes within your group to discuss the message and explore these concepts in Scripture.

1. Based on your personal experience, what are the greatest challenges to unity in a local church or Christian community? How have you seen these challenges overcome?

2. How has your experience of healthy community made your faith stronger? How has it made you a more mature believer in Christ?

3. Do you agree that confessing to one another promotes healing? How does confession facilitate what is required to overcome your struggles with temptation?

4. Part of being a member of Christian community includes sharing in a common goal to spread the gospel and advance God's kingdom. What are some ways that you are partnering with others in your church or small group to reach others for Christ?

5. How well do you know your spiritual gifts and personal strengths within the body of Christ? How have you exercised the gifts that you know you possess?

6. Based on what you've been thinking and processing, why do you believe community to be necessary for both war and rest?

RESPOND

Take a few minutes after your group discussion time to explore the concepts of focus and unity. First, review the questions listed below and write out your responses. Then pair up with someone in your group and spend a few minutes comparing your notes. After you have each had a turn to share, think of ways that you can pray for one another outside of the group time.

What do you enjoy most about your Christian community?

What is your greatest struggle in being part of a community of believers?

What is one way God is calling you to contribute to your community?

PRAY

Conclude your session by sharing any requests you would like the group to lift up in prayer. Thank God for the ways that you have experienced fellowship, encouragement, and healing in past Christian communities as well as those you are presently enjoying. Ask the Lord for protection against the Enemy as you seek to grow closer to other believers and to trust them with what's going on inside your heart. If you are not in healthy community right now, allow God's Spirit to guide you to the place where you can contribute, grow, and thrive.

PERSONAL STUDY

Continue exploring the concepts that you discussed during this week's group meeting by engaging in the following exercises for your personal study time. Be sure to write down any key points that stand out to you so you can share at the next meeting.

CONNECT

Check in with your group members during the upcoming week and continue the discussion you had with them at your last gathering. Grab coffee or dinner or reach out by text and share what's going on in your heart. Use the following questions to help guide your conversation.

How has being part of this group and connecting with others helped you to grow in your faith? What—or who—in particular has encouraged you to draw closer to God?

Have you recently struggled to forgive someone else for an offense against you? If so, how has this struggle hindered your relationship with God?

God's Word tells us, "Confess your sins to each other and pray for each other so that you may be healed" (James 5:16). When have you witnessed the benefits of doing this in your life?

REFLECT

Whether you are part of a committed group of believers or are seeking one, it is important to focus on what you can contribute rather than just what you hope to receive. Envying the roles or gifts of others only weakens your ability to resist temptation and drains your energy when you resent them. Instead, embrace the areas of service where you can step up and give your best, regardless of how you think those gifts compare to others. Toward this goal, read the following passage and use the questions that follow to aid in your reflection.

Just as a body, though one, has many parts, but all its many parts form one body, so it is with Christ. For we were all baptized by one Spirit so as to form one body—whether Jews or Gentiles, slave or free—and we were all given the one Spirit to drink. Even so the body is not made up of one part but of many.

Now if the foot should say, "Because I am not a hand, I do not belong to the body," it would not for that reason stop being part of the body. And if the ear should say, "Because I am not an eye, I do not belong to the body," it would not for that reason stop being part of the body. If the whole body were an eye, where would the sense of hearing be? If the whole body were an ear, where would the sense of smell be? But in fact God has placed the parts in the body, every one of them, just as he wanted them to be. If they were all one part, where would the body be? As it is, there are many parts, but one body.

The eye cannot say to the hand, "I don't need you!" And the head cannot say to the feet, "I don't need you!" On the contrary, those parts of the body that seem to be weaker are indispensable, and the parts that we think are less honorable we treat with special honor. And the parts that are unpresentable are treated with special modesty, while our presentable parts need no special treatment. But God has put the body together, giving greater honor to the parts that lacked it, so that there should be no division in the body, but that its parts should have equal concern for each other. If one part suffers, every part suffers with it; if one part is honored, every part rejoices with it.

Now you are the body of Christ, and each one of you is a part of it.

1 CORINTHIANS 12:12–27

How has God equipped you presently to serve the body of Christ? What experiences in your life have provided skill, insight, and expertise as you serve in this capacity?

Based on what you know about your gifts and abilities, how effectively are you serving your current community? How could you give more of who God has uniquely created you to be?

What can you do in the next week to strengthen unity in your community of believers? How can you involve others to help in this endeavor?

WORSHIP

One of the important ways believers help one another in the Body of Christ is to share their burdens and encourage them through trials and temptations. An unexpected call or text, a small gift, or an act of service can lighten the load and remind them that they are not alone in whatever circumstances they are facing. This kind of compassionate, other-centered attitude goes a long way in building unity in the communion of saints. As you reflect on your role in serving others, read the following passage and answer the questions below.

> *Therefore if you have any encouragement from being united with Christ, if any comfort from his love, if any common sharing in the Spirit, if any tenderness and compassion, then make my joy complete by being like-minded, having the*

same love, being one in spirit and of one mind. Do nothing out of selfish ambition or vain conceit. Rather, in humility value others above yourselves, not looking to your own interests but each of you to the interests of the others.

PHILIPPIANS 2:1–4

When was the last time someone blessed you by their kind words, thoughtful service, or generous gift? When was the last time you blessed someone in this way?

Based on this passage, why is humility essential to your ability to serve others? How does humility contribute to the unity of the group?

How often do you serve others without actually expecting anything in return? What causes you to struggle with your expectations?

How does serving others with humility foster your own peace and rest? How would you describe your feelings when you know you've given your best to serve someone else?

DEEPER

The Christian life isn't just about not getting dirty with the sin of the world. We avoid destruction so we can accomplish our mission and do good in the world. We need community to do this. We want to live united, "with one mind striving side by side for the faith of the gospel" (Philippians 1:27). We strive together. Not against each other, but on the same team, striving together for the same ultimate goal. But we sometimes get that mixed up.

Several years ago, a buddy invited me to play a new military-style video game that his company had developed. We were to work as a team to rescue some hostages. At one point when I moved my character forward, my controls went dead.

"I think your game is glitchy," I said.

"No," my buddy replied, "I think I just shot you in the back of the head."

Well. We are never going to accomplish our mission if we keep taking shots at each other, are we?

Sometimes we are great with having friends as long as we excel in areas we deem important. As long as I'm more athletic, attractive, popular, fashionable, or successful, I will be your friend. We impede our ability to work as a team because we are too focused on our individual stats. We are meant to struggle, not against each other, but alongside each other!

We need community to challenge one another, sharpen one another, and spur one another on toward love and good deeds. We need great minds helping us understand the more complex elements of our faith. We need women and men with pastoral gifts and counseling skills to help us navigate our own deep emotional waters. We need great organizers to rally us to accomplish grander goals than any of us could tackle on our own. *We need us.*

— FROM CHAPTER 11 OF *REST & WAR*

When are times that you have been tempted to take "shots" at other believers?

Why is striving for "individual stats" so detrimental to building unity?

What is one practical way that you could challenge, sharpen, and spur on another person in your community toward love and good deeds?

For Next Week: Before your group's final session, read or review the remaining chapters in *Rest & War*. Pay special attention to what you read about living in the power of the Holy Spirit.

SESSION SIX

KEEP IN STEP

Since we live by the Spirit, let us keep in step with the Spirit.

GALATIANS 5:25

WELCOME

A while back, the power steering went out in my car as I was driving through the center of Washington, DC. This was not good. With the slow speeds and frequent stops necessary for city driving, I lacked the momentum that helped move the wheels as I turned the steering wheel. Suddenly, the simple act of making a turn took an enormous amount of effort. Even using all my formidable muscles and impressive bodyweight, I still made wide turns that drifted into oncoming traffic, which was obviously a problem for me and the surrounding drivers!

You see, a powerless driver is a dangerous driver. I was a threat to myself and others. Finally, I had to admit that to get where I needed to go, I needed a source of strength beyond my own capacities. The same principle holds true for our spiritual lives.

When Jesus commissioned his disciples to go forth and spread the good news of God's grace available through His finished work on the cross, he began by saying, in essence, "Don't attempt to do anything yet!" He instructed them to wait until the empowering presence of the Spirit of God invaded their lives. Then and only then, with the intimate and animating presence of God's Spirit working inside them, could they accomplish the spiritual work that Jesus had called them to do.

The same is true for you and me. The Spirit of God moved into our hearts on the day of our conversion, and we need his presence and power to truly live the spiritual lives God calls us to live. So, before we launch out from this study, we need to understand the empowering presence of God's Holy Spirit.

SHARE

Before we jump into today's session, take a few minutes to share any insights you have from last week's personal study. Then, to get things started, discuss one of the following questions:

> What comes to mind when you think of the Holy Spirit? How would you describe him to someone who is not familiar with the Bible?

— *or* —

> How would you describe the way the Holy Spirit works in a person's life? How can you know when he is actively at work?

READ

Invite someone to read aloud the following passage. Listen for fresh insights as you hear the verses being read and then discuss the questions that follow.

> *"But very truly I tell you, it is for your good that I am going away. Unless I go away, the Advocate will not come to you; but if I go, I will send him to you. When he comes, he will prove the world to be in the wrong about sin and righteousness and judgment: about sin, because people do not believe in me; about righteousness, because I am going to the Father, where you can see me no longer; and about judgment, because the prince of this world now stands condemned. I have much more to say to you, more than you can now bear. But when he, the Spirit of truth, comes, he will guide you into all the truth. He will not speak on his own; he will speak only what he hears, and he will tell you what is yet to come. He will glorify me because it is from me that he will receive what he will make known to you. All that belongs to the Father is mine. That is why I said the Spirit will receive from me what he will make known to you."*
>
> JOHN 16:7–15

Jesus spoke these words to his disciples to prepare them for his departure from this world. What does Jesus say the Holy Spirit will "prove to the world"?

What does Jesus say the Holy Spirit would do in the disciples' lives when he arrived?

WATCH

Play the video segment for session six (use the streaming video access provided on the inside front cover). As you watch, use the following outline to record any thoughts or concepts that stand out to you.

To experience spiritual growth and fulfillment, we need to be rightly related to the Spirit of God. We need the power of the Holy Spirit dwelling in us to elevate, empower, and equip us as we engage in war and seek rest. Without the Spirit as our power source, we will ultimately fail.

In the Old Testament, the Hebrew word for spirit is *ruach*, the same word as *wind* or *breath*. This also refers to the way God breathed life into his human creations, Adam and Eve.

When Adam and Eve disobeyed God, the consequences were disastrous. Not only were their offspring infected with sin, but all humans now also face death. When we die, we return to dust, no longer animated by the intimate presence of God inside our mortal bodies. The tragedy recorded in Genesis reveals that we need this divine breath in order to live.

God gave his people laws and commandments so they could have a relationship with him, but they repeatedly failed and strayed from him. Even when they were willing to obey, they lacked the power in their spirit to love him with their whole hearts and actions (see Ezekiel 36–37).

In Jesus' encounter with the Jewish leader Nicodemus, he explained the role of the Holy Spirit and the necessity of being born again—of being born of the Spirit (see John 3:5–8). Like the power of the wind, you cannot see the Holy Spirit, but you can witness his power in your life.

The Bible says that after Jesus rose victorious over the grave, "he breathed on [his disciples] and said, 'Receive the Holy Spirit' " (John 20:22). Jesus was returning the "wind" they had lost. His death on the cross removed the barrier of sin—a means to an end—so the Holy Spirit could return the animating presence of God inside the people again.

There are three ways that we can know we are being led by the Holy Spirit. First, his guidance will be *consistent* with Scripture. Second, his guidance will be *community-driven*. Third, his guidance will yield certain good *fruit* in our lives (see Galatians 5:22–23).

In order to win the war and experience rest, we need the Spirit of God to blow through our lives. If we want to live in the Spirit, we must walk by the Spirit and keep in step with him.

DISCUSS

Take a few minutes within your group to discuss the message and explore these concepts in Scripture.

1. When has the Holy Spirit given you a breath of fresh air or a sense of refreshment that helped you persevere through a hard day?

2. Why is God's breath of life essential for our bodies to remain alive? Why is the Holy Spirit essential for our forgiveness and sanctification?

3. Think about a situation where you weren't enough—where you knew you could not accomplish something without God's help and he did. How did the Holy Spirit empower you during that time?

4. Why was Nicodemus confused by Jesus' explanation of what was required to see the kingdom of heaven? What might Nicodemus have been expecting from Jesus?

5. Why did Jesus have to remove the barrier of sin in order for us to have access to his Spirit? How did his death on the cross open the way for us to relate directly to God?

6. Do you agree with the three criteria—(1) consistent with Scripture, (2) community-driven guidance, (3) yields good fruit—that indicates the Holy Spirit is at work? Why or why not?

RESPOND

Take a few minutes after your group discussion time to explore the three criteria outlined in this week's teaching—consistency with Scripture, community-driven guidance, and yielding good fruit—that indicate the Holy Spirit is at work in your life. Use the following questions to help you review what you learned and discern when he is speaking to you.

CRITERIA 1: CONSISTENT WITH SCRIPTURE
Read John 14:26. What does this say about the Holy Spirit?

Discerning the voice of the Holy Spirit requires you to become familiar with God's Word. What steps are you currently taking to do this in your life?

CRITERIA 2: COMMUNITY-DRIVEN GUIDANCE
Read Ephesians 4:3–6. What does this passage say about the Holy Spirit?

The Holy Spirit will always compel you to love, encourage, and serve others. How might he be leading you to be more involved in your church and use your gifts?

CRITERIA 3: YIELDS GOOD FRUIT

Read Galatians 5:22–23. What does this passage say about the Holy Spirit?

The fruit of the Holy Spirit is his to give—not yours to create. Where do you see evidence that this fruit is being produced in your life?

PRAY

Conclude this final session by sharing one thing you are especially thankful for, one need you want lifted up in prayer, and one hope you have for the group. Thank God for sending his Holy Spirit to guide you, challenge you, and empower you to battle well. Ask for protection from the Enemy and the various temptations he will send your way as you implement these strategies that you have learned. Pray for wisdom and discernment as you further God's work in this world.

PERSONAL STUDY

Continue exploring the concepts that you discussed during this week's group meeting by engaging in the following exercises for your personal study time. Consider sharing these insights with your group members in the days and weeks following the conclusion of this study.

CONNECT

Check in with your group one last time to discuss what you've learned and celebrate what God has done during the past six sessions. Grab coffee or dinner or reach out by text and share what's going on in your heart. Try to make sure that everyone in your group hears from someone else. Reflect on the questions below on what you've learned about engaging in rest and war.

In what areas of your life do you feel stronger and more equipped to experience victory? How has the group experience contributed to this?

How has the way you relate to God and spend time with him changed since completing this study? How has cultivating your devotion with him drawn you closer to him?

How would you describe what it means to live in, and walk by, the Spirit? How has your experience of God's Spirit in your life changed over the course of this study?

REFLECT

Catching your breath spiritually is often a good idea whenever you complete a study, project, or goal. Pausing to rest allows you to see how you have grown and where God may be leading you next. With these benefits in mind, flip back through your notes, questions, and reflections that you've written, both during your group meetings as well as between sessions. Then answer the following questions as you evaluate your overall experience and its impact.

When looking back through your notes and reflections, what stands out most to you? Are there consistent themes or threads you see running throughout your experiences in the six sessions?

How has your relationship with God changed during this study? Where do you see evidence of this in your notes, answers, and written reflections? In your actions?

How has your spiritual focus become sharper and clearer since you started this study? What have you learned about how to focus on your priorities that wasn't clear to you before? What have you learned about God and how you relate to him?

What passage from God's Word has empowered you the most to overcome temptations and engage in war and rest? Why do you think this truth from the Bible means so much to you?

WORSHIP

Whenever you complete a study, project, or goal, it is also a good idea to take a few moments to thank God for all the work he has done in your life. Today, read the psalm below—or another favorite psalm of your own choosing—and offer gratitude to God for how he has used this study to help you become a stronger spiritual warrior anchored in his peace and protection. Use the questions that follow to enhance your time of reflection and praise.

> *I will extol the LORD at all times;*
> *his praise will always be on my lips.*
> *I will glory in the LORD;*
> *let the afflicted hear and rejoice.*
> *Glorify the LORD with me;*
> *let us exalt his name together.*
>
> *I sought the LORD, and he answered me;*
> *he delivered me from all my fears.*

Those who look to him are radiant;
    their faces are never covered with shame.
This poor man called, and the LORD heard him;
    he saved him out of all his troubles.
The angel of the LORD encamps around those who fear him,
    and he delivers them.

Taste and see that the LORD is good;
    blessed is the one who takes refuge in him.

PSALM 34:1-8

What are the benefits of extolling the Lord "at all times"? How does gratitude help you overcome temptations and focus your attention on cultivating devotion with God?

During the course of this study, for what or whom have you been especially grateful? Why?

What have you learned or experienced about God's character that you weren't aware of prior to this study? How has this new knowledge strengthened your faith?

DEEPER

At the beginning of this study, I told the story of hiking up Longs Peak with my friend. Let me tell you the rest of the story of our misadventures. Once our mountaineer guide began to show us how to breathe properly to accommodate for the lack of oxygen, we fixed our eyes on him and matched the rhythm of our breathing with his. As we did, a marvelous change occurred.

My headache began to subside. My nausea went away. My limbs felt less like dead weights. Our guide then said resolutely, "C'mon. Let's go to the top."

I took my first step and faltered again. "I don't think I have what it takes," I admitted. "I'm sorry." Then came a moment I have thought about often in my twenty-plus years of life since. He leaned in close and said to me, "Grip the back of my belt. You hold on to me, and your friend will hold on to you. I will stamp out footprints in the snow, and when I step up, I'll pull you up with me. I will lead you to the top of this mountain."

I followed his instruction, and sure enough, when he rose up, his power provided what I needed to take my next step. When he rose, I rose. Within a few short minutes, we stood atop one of the highest points in North America and looked down on clouds.

No matter how spiritually in shape we may feel, we will have moments when we are depleted. God's calling on our lives is simply too high to ascend by our own efforts. If we are going to live the victorious lives he demands, we need his supernatural guidance and power.

If we live by the Spirit, let us also walk by the Spirit. True spirituality looks like constant dependence.

— FROM CHAPTER 15 OF *REST & WAR*

How has the Holy Spirit been leading you to adapt to your "new atmosphere"?

In what area of your life right now do you need to follow the Holy Spirit's footprints?

In what area of life do you need the Holy Spirit to provide your "second wind"?

RHYTHMS OF A WELL-FOUGHT LIFE

REST & WAR

AUTHORED BY BEN STUART

LEADER'S GUIDE

Thank you for your willingness to lead a small group through this study. What you have chosen to do is valuable and will make a great difference in the lives of others. The rewards of being a leader are different from those of participating, and we hope that as you lead you will find your own walk with Jesus deepened by the experience.

Rest & War is a six-session Bible study built around video content and small-group interaction. As the group leader, imagine yourself as the host of a party. Your job is to take care of your guests by managing the behind-the-scenes details so that as your guests arrive, they can focus on one another and on the interaction around the topic for that week.

Your role as the group leader is not to answer all the questions or reteach the content—the video, book, and study guide will do most of that work. Your job is to guide the experience and cultivate your small group into a connected and engaged community. This will make it a place for members to process, question, and reflect—not necessarily receive more instruction.

There are several elements in this leader's guide that will help you as you structure your study and reflection time, so be sure to follow along and take advantage of each one.

BEFORE YOU BEGIN

Before your first meeting, make sure the group members have a copy of this study guide. Alternately, you can hand out the study guides at your first meeting and give the members some time to look over the material and ask any preliminary questions. Also make sure they are aware that they have access to the videos at any time through the streaming code provided on the inside front cover. During your first meeting, send a sheet of paper around the room and have the members write down their name, phone number, and email address so you can keep in touch with them during the week.

Generally, the ideal size for a group is eight to ten people, which will ensure that everyone has enough time to participate in discussions. If you have more people, you might want to break up the main group into smaller subgroups. Encourage those who show up at the first meeting to commit to attending the duration of the study, as this will help the group members get to know one another, create stability for the group, and help you know how to best prepare each week.

Each of the sessions begins with an opening reflection. The questions that follow in the "Share" section serve as an icebreaker to get the group members thinking about the general topic at hand. Some people may want to tell a long story in response to one of these questions, but the goal is to keep the answers brief. Ideally, you want everyone in the group to get a chance to answer, so try to keep the responses to a minute or less. If you have talkative group members, say up front that everyone needs to limit their answer to one minute.

Give the group members a chance to answer, but also tell them to feel free to pass if they wish. With the rest of the study, it's generally not a good idea to have everyone answer every question—a free-flowing discussion is more desirable. But with the opening icebreaker-type questions, you can go around the circle. Encourage shy people to share, but don't force them.

At your first meeting, let the group members know each session contains a personal study section that they can use to reflect more on the content during the week. While this is an optional exercise, it will help the members cement the concepts presented during the group study time and encourage them to spend time each day in God's Word. Let them know that if they choose to do so, they can watch the video for the following week by accessing the streaming code found on the inside front cover of their studies. Invite them to bring any questions and insights they uncovered while reading to your next meeting, especially if they had a breakthrough moment or didn't understand something.

WEEKLY PREPARATION

As the leader, there are a few things you should do to prepare for each meeting:

> *Read through the session.* This will help you to become more familiar with the content and know how to structure the discussion times.

> *Decide how the videos will be used.* Determine whether you want the members to watch the videos ahead of time (via the streaming access code found on the inside front cover) or together as a group.

➤ *Decide which questions you want to discuss.* Based on the amount and length of group discussion, you may not be able to get through all the questions, so choose four to five that you definitely want to cover.

➤ *Be familiar with the questions you want to discuss.* When the group meets, you'll be watching the clock, so you want to make sure you are familiar with the questions you have selected. In this way, you'll ensure you have the material more deeply in your mind than your group members.

➤ *Pray for your group.* Pray for your group members throughout the week and ask God to lead them as they study his Word.

In many cases, there will be no one "right" answer to the question. Answers will vary, especially when the group members are being asked to share their personal experiences.

STRUCTURING THE DISCUSSION TIME

As the group leader, it is up to you to keep track of the time and keep things on schedule. You might want to set a timer for each segment so that both you and the group members know when your time is up. (There are some good phone apps for timers that play a gentle chime or other pleasant sound instead of a disruptive noise.)

Don't be concerned if the group members are quiet or slow to share. People are often quiet when they are pulling together their ideas, and this might be a new experience for them. Just ask a question and let it hang in the air for a while until someone speaks up and shares. You can then say, "Thank you. What about others? What came to you when you watched that portion of the teaching?"

Finally, you will need to determine with your group how long you want to meet each week so that you can plan your time accordingly. Generally, most groups like to meet for either ninety minutes or two hours, so you could use one of the following schedules:

SECTION	90 MINUTES	120 MINUTES
WELCOME (members arrive and get settled)	10 minutes	15 minutes
SHARE (discuss one or more of the opening questions for the session)	10 minutes	15 minutes
READ (discuss the questions based on the Scripture reading for the week)	10 minutes	15 minutes
WATCH (watch the teaching material together and take notes)	15 minutes	15 minutes
DISCUSS (discuss the Bible study questions you selected ahead of time)	25 minutes	35 minutes
RESPOND (have everyone go through the closing exercise)	10 minutes	15 minutes
PRAY (pray together as a group and then dismiss)	10 minutes	10 minutes

GROUP DYNAMICS

Leading a group through the *Rest & War* study will prove to be highly rewarding both to you and your group members. But you still may encounter challenges along the way! Discussions can get off track. Group members may not be sensitive to the needs and ideas of others. Some might worry they will be expected to talk about matters that make them feel awkward. Others may express comments that result in disagreements. To help ease this strain on you and the group, consider the following ground rules:

> When someone raises a question or comment that is off the main topic, suggest that you deal with it another time, or, if you feel led to go in that direction, let the group know you will be spending some time discussing it.

> If someone asks a question that you don't know how to answer, admit it and move on. At your discretion, feel free to invite group members to comment on questions that call for personal experience.

> If you find one or two people are dominating the discussion time, direct a few questions to others in the group. Outside the main group time, ask the more dominating members to help you draw out the quieter ones. Work to make them a part of the solution instead of part of the problem.

> When a disagreement occurs, encourage the group members to process the matter in love. Encourage

those on opposite sides to restate what they heard
the other side say about the matter, and then invite
each side to evaluate if that perception is accurate.
Lead the group in examining other Scriptures related to the topic and look for common ground.

When any of these issues arise, encourage your group
members to follow these words from the Bible: "Love one another" (John 13:34), "If it is possible, as far as it depends on
you, live at peace with everyone" (Romans 12:18), "Whatever
is true . . . noble . . . right . . . if anything is excellent or praise-
worthy—think about such things" (Philippians 4:8), and "Be
quick to listen, slow to speak and slow to become angry"
(James 1:19). This will make your group time more rewarding
and beneficial for everyone who attends.

Thank you again for taking the time to lead your group.
You are making a difference in the lives of others and having
an impact on the kingdom of God.

COMPANION BOOK TO ENRICH YOUR STUDY EXPERIENCE

RHYTHMS OF A WELL FOUGHT LIFE

REST & WAR.

BEN STUART

ISBN 9780785248316

Available wherever books are sold

MORE FROM

Harper*Christian* Resources

We hope you enjoyed this Bible study from
HarperChristian Resources.

Find your next Bible study, video series, or ministry training at:
HarperChristianResources.com

YouTube.com/HarperChristianResources

Facebook.com/HarperChristianResources

Instagram.com/HarperChristianResources

Twitter.com/HCResources

——————— OUR MISSION ———————

Equipping people to understand the Scriptures, cultivate spiritual growth,
and live an inspired faith with Bible study and video resources
from today's most trusted voices.

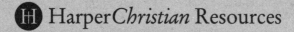

Also Available from Ben Stuart

In this six-session study, Ben Stuart helps you apply the principles in his book *Single, Dating, Engaged, Married* to your life. The study guide includes video notes, group discussion questions, and personal study and reflection materials for in between sessions.

Study Guide
9780310140047

DVD with
Free Streaming Access
9780310140061

Available now at your favorite bookstore,
or streaming video on StudyGateway.com.

W PUBLISHING GROUP

AN IMPRINT OF THOMAS NELSON

It's Not the Height of the Giant ... but the Size of Our God

EXPLORE THE PRINCIPLES IN *GOLIATH MUST FALL* through this six-session video-based study. Each week, pastor Louie Giglio will provide practical steps and biblical principles for how you and your group can defeat the "giants" in your lives like fear, rejection, comfort, anger, or addiction. Includes discussion questions, Bible exploration, and personal study materials for in between sessions.

Available now at your favorite bookstore, or streaming video on StudyGateway.com.

passionpublishing   HarperChristian Resources

Video Study for Your Church or Small Group

In this six-session study, Louie Giglio helps you apply the principles in *Don't Give the Enemy a Seat at Your Table* to your life. The study guide includes video notes, group discussion questions, and personal study materials for in between sessions.

Available now at your favorite bookstore,
or streaming video on StudyGateway.com.

From the Publisher

GREAT STUDIES

ARE EVEN BETTER WHEN THEY'RE SHARED!

Help others find this study:

- Post a review at your favorite online bookseller.

- Post a picture on a social media account and share why you enjoyed it.

- Send a note to a friend who would also love it—or, better yet, go through it with them!

Thanks for helping others grow their faith!